GREENING YOUR OFFICE

This book belongs to
Danielle Tomerlin

Greening Your Office

From Cupboard to Corporation: An A–Z Guide

Jon Clift & Amanda Cuthbert

Chelsea Green Publishing Company
White River Junction, Vermont

First published in 2007 by Green Books, Foxhole, Dartington, Totnes, Devon TQ9 6EB, UK

Interior design concept by Julie Martin jmartin1@btinternet.com

First Chelsea Green printing January, 2008

Printed in Canada.

Text printed on 100-percent postconsumer-waste recycled paper.

10 9 8 7 6 5 4 3 2   08 09 10

DISCLAIMER: The advice in this book is believed to be correct at the time of printing, but the authors and publishers accept no liability for actions inspired by this book.

We would like to thank Ben Brakes of Barclaycard, Simon Clifford of BBC Somerset Sound, the Britannia Building Society, Rory McMullan, author of *Cycling to Work: a beginner's guide*, Paul Ellis of the Ecology Building Society, Amy Sims of Global Action Plan, Ali Clabburn of Liftshare, Matt Criddle of NatureSave, Chris Hillyer of South Hams District Council, and Heather Goringe of Wiggly Wigglers.

Library of Congress Cataloging-in-Publication Data

Clift, Jon.
  Greening your office / Jon Clift and Amanda Cuthbert.
     p. cm.
1. Salvage (Waste, etc.)--Environmental aspects. 2. Waste minimization.
3. Office management--Environmental aspects. 4. Offices--Environmental aspects. 5. Offices--Energy conservation--Citizen participation. 6. Quality of work life. I. Cuthbert, Amanda. II. Title.

  TP995.C57 2008
  333.72--dc22

2007046286

Chelsea Green Publishing Company
P.O. Box 428
White River Junction, VT 05001
(802) 295-6300
www.chelseagreen.com

Contents

GREENING YOUR OFFICE

Introduction

Climate change is happening, due primarily to rising carbon dioxide (CO_2) levels in the atmosphere; we are running out of landfill sites, and using up our natural resources at an alarming rate. Whether you are a managing director or a receptionist, a global corporation or a one-man band, there are things you can do — both as an individual and as an organization — to reduce your carbon footprint and help both the planet and your budget. In writing this book we have concentrated on the administrative side of a business, looking at what can be done to make the office a greener place; there is not space in a book of this kind to address all the things that companies as a whole can do to green up, since they come in many different shapes and sizes and have differing concerns, depending on their nature. However, many of the principles, such as saving energy and water, can be applied to other areas of a business as well as the office.

We have included inspirational examples of those who have greened up and benefited from doing so. If you make just one office practice more environmentally friendly, you will make a difference.

Chapter 1

Why do it?

We spend a large amount of our time in the office, where we use considerable amounts of energy and resources. "Greening the office" will therefore have significant benefits, both environmentally and financially. As many other businesses have experienced, small changes to your office practices and procurements, mostly costing nothing, will reduce the company's expenditure and improve your sales. By being proactive, you stay ahead of impending government legislation, as climate change and mandatory reductions in carbon emissions are being debated. It makes compelling, realistic business sense to green up the office, and helps in our battle with climate change.

There are many arguments for going green in the office:

- Minimize overheads by reducing
  - use of consumables
  - energy costs
  - costs of waste disposal
  - water bills
  - expenditures on office hardware
  - transportation bills
  - parking spaces

- Increase competitiveness by:

  - keeping production costs down as overheads are cut

- improving sales as your green credentials attract new customers
- Improve investment potential: increasing numbers of investors only invest in businesses that have environmentally responsible policies
- Create a feel-good factor in the workplace, encouraging staff retention and recruitment
- Enhance your reputation and brand awareness
- Do your bit to reduce climate change

Whether you are part of a large organization or a one-man band, this book will help you green your office. Even if you do only some of the things suggested in the following chapters, both your business and the environment will benefit.

Chapter 2

Getting people on board

Staff are key to the whole process of greening the office. They are an incredible resource, and if asked, will come up with numerous thoughts and suggestions to minimize waste and reduce energy costs.

From the very beginning they need to be part of the process, involved and informed. It is obviously crucial that senior management are also committed to the process — that they "walk the talk" and lead the way.

With climate change now a factor of life, most people will be eager to help green up the office, especially when they are encouraged to own the process.

Motivate staff and colleagues

If your organization is spread across several sites, you can start small in one of them and spread the plan to the others. Depending on the size of the organization and whether all staff work in one place, there are a number of ways to get the ball rolling:

- A staff suggestion box
- An internal e-mail address
- A "green" bulletin board
- An intranet forum discussion group
- An initial meeting if feasible

Create an "Environmental Taskforce"

Ask for volunteers to set up an "Environmental Taskforce" to involve staff, collate suggestions, and implement realistic ideas. If your organization is large, you will need a coordinator and individuals in each section. If you have a smaller office this could be done by one person.

The environmental taskforce will:

- Monitor current practices: for example, sheets of paper used per week, number of staff traveling by car, number of computers left on standby each night, number of lights left on in the office, etc.

- Set realistic targets. SMART targets are great to keep in mind: **S**pecific, **M**easurable, **A**ttainable, **R**ealistic, **T**ime-bound

- Start with "easy hit" targets (e.g., reducing paper consumption, recycling ink cartridges, switching off monitors, switching lights off when not needed)

- Consider appropriate incentives: a carrot is better than a stick!

- Nominate individuals within the team to monitor progress on each project being tackled

- Keep the communication flowing. It's crucial to keep everybody well informed and up to date regarding targets set, achievements, and any problems encountered

- Let the outside world know what's happening. Use the process to everyone's advantage; use in-house journals, the press, your Web site, and local TV and radio — and tell your customers. Greening up is great PR

- Celebrate success. Think up intriguing and innovative ways to mark milestones

- Keep the momentum going. Once "easy hit" targets have been achieved and the workforce is motivated and on-board, try for more ambitious (but still SMART) targets

- Beware of a false sense of completion — while a few simple "quick wins" are great for morale, they can and frequently do make people think that the job is done

Every individual act makes a difference. Whether you work from home or are part of a global corporation, your actions big and small will contribute to the fight against climate change.

Chapter 3

A–Z Guide

Adhesives – *see Glues, Solvents*

Aerosols

Where possible avoid aerosols: both the propellant and the contents could damage your health. Buy environmentally friendly products that come in liquid form, and wipe or spray using a pump spray.

Air Conditioning – *see also Lighting, Office Equipment, Plants*

Running an air-conditioning unit adds on average about 50% to your annual electricity bill.

Air conditioning (the cooling of your office air to make it slightly colder than the outside temperature) is extremely energy hungry; it adds to your electricity bills as well as increases greenhouse gas emissions.

Don't switch it on; reduce the need for air conditioning by:

Reducing internal heat sources Most of the energy consumed by conventional light bulbs is released as heat, which is very inefficient. Change your light bulbs to low-energy ones — remove this heat source and reduce your energy bill at the same time (see **Lighting** below).

Most conventional office equipment, from computers to photocopiers, also produces heat when operating, further warming your office air. Switch machines off when not needed or put them on standby. Consider using the "traffic light system" for your office equipment: red — do not turn off; amber — put on standby; green — turn off (see **Office Equipment**).

Shading your windows Preventing the sun's rays from entering your office will help prevent the air in your office from warming up. Curtains and blinds inside the office help considerably. However, it is most effective to shade the windows externally by fitting shutters or awnings, which can be put away when not required.

If your office is on the ground floor, consider creating shade by growing plants around, above, and over your windows. There are many fast-growing beautiful plants that will add a new dimension to your office space and be a pleasure to watch throughout the seasons (see **Plants** below).

Ventilating naturally — open the windows! Experiment with opening various windows to produce a pleasant cooling breeze; on all but the stillest day it is possible to generate natural ventilation.

Air Fresheners – *see also Aerosols*

Open windows rather than using air fresheners, as many contain potentially dangerous chemicals that could damage your health. Locally grown flowers and plants provide natural fragrances and color in the office — a much more pleasant alternative.

Air Travel – *see Flights*

Ballpoint Pens – *see Pens*

Bathrooms – *see Restrooms*

Batteries

Used batteries are hazardous waste and must not go to a landfill. Have a collection point for batteries and find out how to recycle or dispose of them.

Bleach – *see also Cleaning, Kitchens*

Avoid using chlorine-based bleach, including toilet deodorizers and household bleach, as it can cause damage to health and the environment.

Bicycles – *see Cycling*

Binding Machines – *see also Office Equipment*

Most binding machines are only used infrequently and therefore should be switched off when not in use. Put a "green" sticker on them if you adopt the traffic-light-system group (see **Office Equipment**). However, if your office uses a thermal binder frequently and it takes a while to warm up, then it might warrant an "amber" traffic-light symbol.

Choose a comb binder, which does not need electricity, if possible.

Buses

Buses are one of the most energy-efficient ways to travel — use them where possible.

Calendars

Why not use a computer program for your planning? Most have calendar software programed in; upload to a Web page if others need to access it.

Calculators

Use solar-powered where possible, rather than plug-in models.

Cans

If aluminum cans are used in your office, make sure you have a recycling plan for them; find out if there is a redemption center in your area, or a charity that would welcome the money it could raise from your donated aluminum.

Carbon Dioxide

Carbon dioxide (CO_2) is the main greenhouse gas contributing to climate change. Levels of CO_2 in the atmosphere are rising dramatically, and we urgently need to reduce our CO_2 emissions in order to avoid catastrophic climate change.

Carbon Footprint

Your carbon footprint is the measure of the amount of carbon dioxide your activities add to the atmosphere. Carbon dioxide (CO_2) is the main greenhouse gas contributing to climate change. Surprisingly, many items — from apples to cars — can have a carbon footprint too, especially if they have been flown thousands of miles or if energy has been used in their production. Your purchasing choices affect your overall carbon footprint.

Carbon Offsetting

Carbon offsetting is the principle whereby the carbon emissions created by activities such as flying or driving can be theoretically "offset" by donating money to various "green" projects such as tree planting or renewable-energy projects. The notional CO_2 that these projects possibly "save" from going into the atmosphere or reduce at some possible future date gives the perception that people can carry on polluting and buy their way out of the problem. It is preferable to cut emissions in the first place, and only to consider credible carbon offsetting as a last resort.

Cardboard – *see Packing materials*

Car Fleets – *see Fleet Cars*

Carpets – *see also Flooring*

If you are replacing a carpet, consider purchasing one made from natural materials that come from a renewable source rather than a man-made fiber derived from oil. Examples such as wool and sisal, jute and coconut coir, not only look and smell good but are hard-wearing too. In noncarpeted areas, such as the kitchen, use eco-friendly flooring: cork tiles wear well and insulate the floor. Does the carpet really need replacing — could it be steam cleaned instead?

Car Pools – *see also Cars*

If you have to take your car to work, can you share your car with others making a similar journey?

Car Purchase – *see Company Cars*

Cars – *see also Cycling, Company Cars*

Driving is responsible for 20% of our CO_2 emissions within the United States, with half of that coming from our cars.

We urgently need to use our cars less, thereby reducing CO_2 and other pollutants and reducing road congestion, as well as saving ourselves money and getting fitter in the process.

Many of us are wedded to our cars, and require considerable enticements to leave them at home and come to work another

way. But once car owners are aware of the personal, social, and financial advantages, many become passionately committed to greener ways of traveling.

There are many advantages for both staff and the company to promote greener ways to commute, such as:

- Saving money, and in some cases even earning extra
- Reducing the need for car-parking space
- Reducing business miles
- Having healthier and more motivated people
- Reducing CO_2 emissions

Your objectives will be to reduce single-car occupancy and promote alternative forms of transportation, both for commuting to work and for other business trips.

There are many things you can do to encourage people to switch to alternative means of commuting:

- Subsidize bus/rail/subway tickets. The costs will be significantly less than the annual costs of maintaining car-parking spaces
- Provide easily accessible information about public transportation with maps showing biking and walking routes, timetables, and contact names via your green notice board, e-mail, your local area network (LAN) or intranet.
- Approach your local bus company (armed with facts and figures) to see if they will reroute a bus at key times if your office is not well served by public transportation
- Create good facilities for cyclists, secure bike storage, showers with lockers, free breakfasts, and financial incentives for cycling to work

- Set up a "bike buddy" and/or "walking buddy" database through e-mail, your local area network (LAN), the company Web site/intranet, or bulletin board
- Organize bike purchasing through your company, thereby saving about half the total costs of the bike
- Set up weekly visits by a "bike doctor" who will repair and maintain bikes

For those who have difficulty changing their means of transportation, you can reduce the number of cars coming to the office by:

- Promoting carpooling, with priority parking spaces for those who participate
- Setting up a carpooling database on the company Web site/intranet, local area network (LAN), by e-mail, or on a bulletin board for potential car poolers with a guarantee of a free taxi should their ride not show up
- Reviewing your business-mileage allowance for cars. Set a flat rate for all cars based on the most fuel-efficient, regardless of engine size
- Organizing occasional car-free days, with incentives and rewards

Reduce the need to travel:

- Assess potential conference venues and prioritize them according to accessibility by public transportation
- Review your business travel — is the visit really necessary?
- Investigate using video conferencing — very cheap with PC-mounted cameras, and it can be done from any workstation
- Ensure that all visitors are made aware of public transportation links and of your policy to reduce car use
- Can some employees work from home? Just once a week will substantially reduce staff commuting

- If people get in their cars to go and buy their lunch, consider an in-house cafeteria, or a restaurant within walking distance, or find a sandwich-delivery company, or organize a bus if you have sufficient numbers

Celebrations – *see also Christmas*

When you are ready to celebrate your success, make sure you do so in an environmentally friendly way, for example, by using:

- Locally grown flowers
- Real glasses rather than plastic ones
- Locally grown food and drink

Chemicals – *see also Cleaning, Furniture, Glues*

Reduce the amount of toxic chemicals in the office where possible, whether in cleaning materials, furniture, fabrics, glues, or inks. There are many environmentally friendly products available.

Christmas – *see also Celebrations*

Get a Christmas tree in a pot that can be planted in a garden and used the following year. Recycle all greeting cards, send e-mail cards, or even make your own office cards. Buy "green" presents, and make sure as much as possible of any food and drink you buy is organic or locally grown.

Christmas Cards – *see Christmas*

Cleaning – *see also Aerosols, Chemicals*

Products used to clean offices can be toxic, with chemicals and solvents that could damage your health (for example, bleach) and pollute the environment; check out the ingredients in your soaps and detergents, and avoid phosphates — there are many environmentally friendly cleaning products available.

Where there is a cleaning contract, it can be reviewed for opportunities to change to products that are safe for the cleaners, those who work in the office, and the environment.

Coffee – *see also Organic, Tea*

Buy and use organic coffee if possible — less carbon dioxide is emitted in organic farming. Organic produce is readily available and promotes a much more pleasant and safe way of farming; and how about using organic milk with your coffee?

If you use "real" coffee, why not compost the coffee grounds afterwards?

Commuting – *see also Bicycles, Buses, Cars, Car Pools, Ride Sharing*

Leave your car at home; use public transportation, walk, or cycle to work instead. See **Cars** above for more information.

Compact Discs

Use rewritable CDs rather than nonreusable CDs. Can you use a thumb drive or memory stick or external hard drive? Recycle your CDs and DVDs.

Company Cars – *see Cars, Fleet Cars*

Composting

Instead of throwing all leftover food, tea bags, and coffee grounds into the trash, why not set up a composting system to prevent these organic materials from going to the landfill? When these materials decompose in a landfill they produce methane, an extremely potent greenhouse gas. Even if your office is not on the ground floor, there are various methods now available to allow you to compost your organic waste. The gardeners in your office will eagerly take the finished product home.

Photo of Bokashi bin courtesy of Wiggly Wigglers

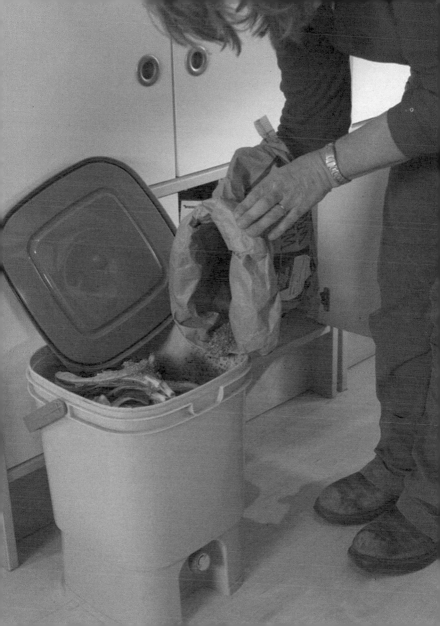

There are different kinds of composting systems. If you want to be able to compost all types of food waste, including meat and fish products, make sure you purchase the correct type. You will need to choose one according to where it is going to be located.

Some garden space required

- Tumblers – available through garden centers and online
- Green Johannas – the "Rolls Royce" of the plastic compost bin (the manufacturers claim you need no composting experience) **www.greenjohanna.se**
- Digesters such as the "Green Cone" dispose of the waste but do not produce compost **www.greencone.com**

No garden space required

- Bokashi system – uses bacteria that thrive without air to ferment the material. No unpleasant smells are produced, and it can be used indoors.
- Wormeries – this system is great fun but requires a little more effort; the worms within it need looking after! However, it is most rewarding. The worms eat food waste, paper, and cardboard, producing "worm castings," a very valuable plant fertilizer.

Computer Screens – *see Computers*

Computers – *see also Office Equipment*

A computer left on overnight uses 1 Kwh of electricity; if 1,000 people turned off their computers when they went home, they would save 180 metric tons of CO_2 emissions every year.

Office computers tend to stay switched on, quietly consuming electricity throughout every working day. Surveys have shown that many office computers are never switched off, because either the operator can't be bothered or is unaware of the need.

- Turn computers off when not in use, especially at the end of the day. It's an easy task for your green-office campaign, and boosts morale and momentum. Just turning off computers for evenings and weekends will cut their running costs by more than two-thirds

- Set all computers to energy-saving mode so that the screen is switched off if the computer has not been used for more than a few minutes

- Don't be fooled by screen savers — they use as much energy as the normal screen

- Set all computers to switch to "standby" mode when not used for a short while. The power needed to restart is equivalent to only a couple of seconds normal running time

- When replacing computers, compare overall energy use (both running and standby). Check that they have standby or power-down modes

- Flat-screen or LCD monitors consume about one-third of the energy of traditional screens

  Computers are "green" in the "traffic-light system" because they can be switched off when not in use – see **Office Equipment**

When upgrading computers and monitors, give old ones a longer life by selling or giving them to staff for home use, or contact one of numerous commercial organizations or charities that will take your old computers, wipe the hard drive clean, and either sell them or donate them to charities, schools, or for use in developing countries. See **earth911.com** to find out more about computer recycling.

Correction Fluids

Buy correction fluids that do not contain toxic solvents; look for makes that are trichloroethane-free.

Couriers – *see also Deliveries, Mail*

If you use or are considering using couriers to move both paperwork and light objects around a city, consider using a bicycle messenger: they are the ultimate environmentally friendly couriers — they have zero carbon emissions, and are quick and efficient.

For larger parcels or for greater distances check out courier companies that use biofuels or are working to make your delivery carbon neutral by supporting alternative energy and tree-planting projects. Avoid courier companies that use air freight.

Credit Cards

Can your company use a credit card linked to an environmental charity?

Cups – *see also Kettles, Kitchens, Vending Machines, Water, Water Coolers*

Use "real" cups, mugs, and glasses that can be washed, rather than disposable ones. When doing dishes, wait until there are sufficient numbers of mugs to warrant filling the sink. Use an eco-friendly dish-washing liquid, and try to use as little water as possible. Don't keep the water running. Consider purchasing an energy-efficient dishwasher if your office and kitchen is large enough.

If your office uses a water cooler with disposable cups, see if glasses can be used instead.

Curtains

Curtains are good heat insulators, especially if lined with thick materials such as brushed cotton. They can provide shading from direct sunlight during hot summer days and keep heat in during cold winter days and evenings. Draw curtains over windows at night, as they provide insulation and help keep the heat in the room.

When replacing curtains, use natural renewable fibers such as cotton or wool rather than human-made materials made from nonrenewable sources.

Cycling – *see also Cars*

Bikes are a great way to get to work — they are cheap, carbon neutral, easy to park, often quicker than cars, and good exercise.

Bike to work instead of driving your car. Try it for a day a week to start with, and choose days when the weather is fine. You'll save yourself money and become fitter in the process. Break the car habit, reduce your carbon emissions, and add years to your life!

Datebooks – *see also Calendars*

Can you keep your datebook on your computer rather than using a hard copy?

Deliveries – *see also Couriers*

If you have sufficient space, change your ordering so that you order occasional large consignments of consumables rather than ordering small amounts when you need them. The fewer the number of deliveries, the smaller your carbon footprint.

Detergents – *see Cleaning*

DVDs – *see Compact Discs*

Electricity – *see Energy Purchasing, Lighting, Heating, Office Equipment*

Elevators

Don't waste electricity; use the stairs instead. Reduce your carbon footprint and get fitter in the process.

Energy – *see also Air Conditioning, Computers, Energy Purchasing, Heating, Kettles, Lighting, Office Equipment, Photocopiers, Printers, Scanners, Ventilation, Windows*

There are major financial and environmental benefits in reducing your energy consumption. Energy is used to heat your office in the winter, and possibly to keep it cool in the summer. Energy in the form of electricity runs all your office equipment, elevators, lighting, and ventilation. It is a major office expenditure, and can easily be reduced by a few simple actions. See individual topics for specific information.

Energy Star

Where possible buy office equipment with the Energy Star label. This is found on office products that meet or exceed energy efficient guidelines. **www.energystar.gov**

Envelopes

Use envelopes made from recycled paper; these come in as many colors and qualities as virgin paper envelopes and are available from most suppliers. If you use window envelopes, get those with the windows made from cellulose window film, as this can be recycled. Reuse envelopes whenever possible — opening carefully, resealing, and readdressing before use. Many charities sell envelope reuse labels, which can cover up the original address and stamp.

Environmental Taskforce

Those members of the organization who volunteer to lead the environmental improvements to the office (see page 6).

Fair Trade

Primarily an ethical rather than green issue, fair-trade products are purchased directly from the producers or growers, guaranteeing them a better price for their products. The extra premium on these products is reinvested in social or economic development projects.

Fans – *see Air Conditioning*

Filing and Storage

Question whether you need to continue filing and storing paper copies of letters, invoices, reports, and the like. Instead of hard copies, back up electronic versions daily onto external hard drives or CDs. If you do need paper files or folders, buy recycled if possible.

Fleet Cars – *see also Cars*

- When leasing or purchasing fleet cars consider green issues such as CO_2 emissions and miles per gallon
- Keep your fleet maintained and regularly serviced
- Keep your fleet cars longer if possible — do they really need to be replaced so often?
- Give staff training to drive economically
- Encourage staff who drive fleet cars to use public transportation where possible and minimize their fuel consumption

Flights

On average, flying contributes about 10 times as much carbon dioxide to the atmosphere as a similar journey by train.

Ensure that all staff are aware of the environmental damage caused by flying. Make it company policy that all longer business journeys are taken by train rather than plane where possible. Or try to avoid making the journey altogether: investigate using video conferencing (with PC mounted cameras).

Flip Charts

Buy recycled flip charts. Can you reuse your used flip-chart paper for office pads?

Flooring – *see also Carpets, Paints*

Natural products that come from sustainable sources such as wood, cork, bamboo, and linoleum (not vinyl floor coverings, which are human-made) are preferable to human-made products, which pollute your office environment with unpleasant chemicals and are generally derived from oil. Ensure these natural floorings are coated with nontoxic products to keep your office healthy and environmentally friendly.

Flower Miles – *see also Gardens, Plants*

If you buy flowers for the office or for individual staff for special occasions, consider where the flowers have been grown and the method of transportation. The vast bulk of commercial flowers are grown abroad and flown in from countries as distant as Columbia, Kenya, and Israel. Flower air miles damage the environment, contributing to the carbon dioxide levels in our atmosphere and thereby climate change, and the way they are grown is very often harmful to those who work with them and

the local environment. Consider purchasing flowers obtained from local sources, and buy flowers that are in season rather than hothouse-forced ones.

Flowers – *see Plants*

Folders – *see Filing and Storage*

Food

Whether you are purchasing for a canteen or boardroom lunch, or simply want a snack, try and buy locally grown, organic produce where possible and support your local markets. Avoid highly packaged food.

Food Miles – *see also Food, Kitchens*

Food miles are the miles your food has traveled to get from its origin to your plate. The greater the distance, the greater the CO_2 created, and therefore the greater the impact of your food on climate change — especially if it has been freighted by air from its source. Local food, in season, both grown and sold locally, creates the minimum food miles.

Buy locally grown food in season and sold through local markets and co-ops.

Forest Stewardship Council (FSC) – *see also Furniture, Paper*

FSC is a widely used certification for timber and other products that originate from trees that enables the purchaser to be confident that the forest source is managed sustainably and does not contribute to global forest destruction. **www.fscus.org**

Furniture

Furniture made from natural timber rather than chipboard or

MDF (medium density fiberboard) is preferable, as the latter leaches formaldehyde, a chemical that has the potential to damage your health.

When purchasing natural timber products, ensure that the timber used comes from a sustainable source. Look out for the FSC (Forest Stewardship Council) symbol. A good deal of office furniture is thrown out every year — consider buying secondhand or refurbishing your existing furniture, or donating it to charity.

Gardens – *see also Composting, Plants, Rain Barrels*

If your office is on the ground floor and you are fortunate to have some outside space, take full advantage of it. Grow wonderful plants, use them to shade your windows in the summer, and give your office space a third dimension. Pick flowers and foliage to put in your office — a bunch of freshly picked flowers brightens up everybody's day.

Glues – *see also Solvents*

Buy and use vegetable or water-based glues; avoid glues containing toxic solvents such as toluene and xylene. Buy glues from companies that are well informed and only sell environmentally friendly goods.

Ground-Source Heat Pumps – *see Renewable Energy*

Heating – *see also Air Conditioning, Curtains, Insulation*

Simply by turning the thermostat down by 2°F you can reduce your energy bill by 10%.

Heating your office during the winter months is a large proportion of your overall energy bill. The CO_2 generated in producing this heat contributes to climate change; however,

there are many simple actions you can take in your office to reduce your energy use and therefore your carbon footprint.

- Consider turning down the thermostat controlling the temperature of your office by 2°F – you will probably not notice the difference. Research has shown that office staff are generally comfortable at 66°F, so turn down the thermostat incrementally to arrive at this temperature

- Turn radiators off or down in rooms that are only used occasionally, and turn the heating up when needed. Keep these rooms ventilated to prevent condensation and possible mold

- If your radiators are underneath windows, tuck any curtains in behind them to enable the heat to come into the room

- Move furniture away from radiators or heaters, to allow heat to get out into the office

- If possible make sure that your office heating system is set to come on about half an hour before the office will be used in the morning, and to go off about half an hour before the last person leaves in the evening

- Check all the timers, especially for weekends, when the heat can be on for considerably shorter periods and at a much lower temperature; 45°F is sufficient to prevent pipes from freezing in cold weather

- If your office shuts down for a holiday break, adjust the thermostat settings accordingly

- If your office is too hot in the winter months, turn the heat down or off rather than opening windows. If your heat is on, make sure all windows are closed

WARNING Don't block air vents or grates in walls if you have an open gas fire, a boiler with an open flue, or a solid-fuel fire or heater. These need sufficient ventilation to burn properly — otherwise highly poisonous carbon monoxide gas is released.

- Keep external doors shut, and if there are still drafts see if weather stripping can be fitted around doors and over windows; this won't cost very much. But make sure you still have sufficient ventilation — see above

- If there are drafts coming from under skirting boards or through floorboards, see whether gaps can be filled. But make sure you still have sufficient ventilation — see above

- Service your heating system regularly — it will be more efficient and use less energy, saving the company money and reducing your company's contribution to climate change

- If your boiler is due for replacement, consider the most energy-efficient model rather than the cheapest available. As energy prices continue to rise, it will save money and produce less CO_2

- Make sure all radiators have individual thermostats where possible — this will allow you to vary the temperature in different rooms, according to use

- Use plug-in electric heaters such as space heaters, fan heaters, oil-filled radiators, or panel heaters sparingly — they are very expensive to run

Home

Encourage staff to put into practice at home the environmental actions they are taking in the office. There are huge financial savings to be made in the home by doing some simple things: the less energy you use, the smaller your energy bills and the less CO_2 is released, benefitting us all by helping to reduce climate change.

Hydro Power – *see Renewable Energy*

Information Packets – *see Training Manuals*

Ink Cartridges – *see also Deliveries, Ordering*

It is relatively easy to forecast your usage of ink cartridges. Benefit financially and help save the planet by ordering occasional bulk orders rather than frequent small orders when needed. Consider using remanufactured cartridges, or getting them refilled.

There are over 300 million inkjet cartridges thrown away every year in the United States. Most of these could be reused many times by being refilled or remanufactured.

Insulation – *see also Air Conditioning, Curtains, Heating, Windows*

If you are building a new office or refurbishing an existing one, ensure that all walls and the loft or roof spaces are well insulated. This will both prevent heat loss in the winter and keep you cooler in the summer, thereby dramatically reducing your heating and air conditioning costs.

Almost 40% of all the heat used to heat your office escapes through the walls and roof spaces if they are not insulated.

Insurance

There are a limited number of insurance companies that put a percentage of their premium into environmental projects and offer environmental performance reviews.

Invoices

Consider using electronic invoices instead of paper: you can create your invoices as PDF documents and e-mail them to customers.

Junk Mail – *see also Mail Preference Registry*

Send it back in the prepaid envelopes and ask to be removed from the database — trees have been cut down to create this waste. For your own marketing, why not use e-mail?

Kettles – *see also Cups, Coffee, Fair Trade, Kitchens, Water*

Electric kettles consume a surprisingly large amount of electricity, which varies considerably according to the model. When you replace your kettle, choose one with minimum energy consumption. Your kettle will be more efficient if it is kept free of lime scale.

Kettles often heat up more water than is necessary; only boil as much as you need. Many now have an indicator showing the amount of water they contain. Consider an insulated kettle, which will keep any extra water hot until next time.

If your office is large enough, investigate using an electric urn instead of a kettle; you could save considerably on energy used and have hot water for tea and coffee instantly available.

Kitchens – *see also Cleaning, Composting, Cups, Coffee, Fair Trade, Kettles, Milk, Water*

- Set up well-labeled recycling bins in the kitchen for plastic bottles and cans, with another bin for all the lunch waste, tea bags, and coffee grounds, which can go to be composted. To ensure success, pin up a poster to explain where things should go and why

- If the hot tap water is too hot to use, see whether the temperature can be turned down. Don't waste energy heating water only to have to add cold water so that you can use it! Just over 140°F should do it

- Make sure there are no dripping taps. One dripping tap can waste at least 1,500 gallons of water a year

- For heating or defrosting food, a microwave is more energy efficient than a conventional oven

- If your office is large enough, consider purchasing a rated energy-efficient dishwasher rather than washing dishes and cups by hand. Providing the dishwasher is full and its economy or "eco" mode is used, Energy Star–rated dishwashers are surprisingly frugal with both water and energy usage

- Use environmentally friendly cleaning products for both washing dishes and cleaning the kitchen area. There are several well-known brands available

- If you need paper towels, buy recycled

Labels

Why not print directly onto the envelopes and minimize the use of labels?

Landfill

Space for landfill is fast running out. Recycle as much as you can.

Laminators – *see also Office Equipment*

Most laminators are only used infrequently, and consequently should be switched off when not in use. They will therefore have a "green" sticker on them if you adopt the traffic-light system (see **Office Equipment**).

However, if your office uses a laminator frequently and it takes a while to warm up, it might warrant an "amber" traffic-light symbol. If replacing a laminator, buy one that shuts off after a period of inactivity.

Laptops

If you are replacing a computer, consider a laptop because they are much more energy efficient.

Lighting

This is one of those "easy hit" targets — with a simple "switch off" campaign you can get most of the staff involved and motivated.

- Replace all conventional light bulbs with energy-efficient light bulbs, which last about 12 times longer than ordinary bulbs and consume about 1/5 of the energy

- Label all light switches to say which lights they operate, with a reminder to switch off when not needed

- Encourage staff to use natural lighting when available

- Evaluate the office layout, and consider moving furniture to maximize natural lighting

- Don't use more lights than you actually need

- In areas not in constant use, such as restrooms, hallways, stairs, and storerooms, replace the light switches with movement sensors that switch on the lights only when needed. Timer switches can also be used where appropriate

- Make it clear that it is the responsibility of the last person who leaves the office to ensure all the lights are switched off when he or she leaves. If it is the office cleaners, then raise this with them and their management

- Uplighters, or torchieres, can use high-wattage bulbs that are expensive to run — use energy-efficient spots instead

- Halogen bulbs are not energy efficient; energy-efficient replacement bulbs are now available

- Contrary to popular belief, you save energy if you turn strip lights off when not in use — switch them off!

Energy-efficient light bulbs are cheap to run because they mainly make light rather than heat. Up to 90% of the energy used by traditional incandescent bulbs is wasted in producing heat.

Are you the last person
to leave?
Don’t forget
TURN OFF
ALL THE
LIGHTS
Yale

Local Area Network (LAN) – *see also Paper*

A LAN (office computer network), which enables you to share and send information electronically, is a key tool in the paperless office.

Mail – *see also Couriers, Deliveries, Stamps*

While it is outside your control how the mail is distributed within the United States, when mailing items abroad consider whether they need to go by air mail, or if they could be sent surface mail. Although this takes longer, surface mail (ships or trains rather than planes) will reduce the carbon footprint of your posted items.

Mail Preference Registry

Register with the National Do Not Mail List to reduce your junk mail. **www.directmail.com**

Marker Pens – *see Pens*

Milk – *see also Coffee, Kitchens, Tea, Fair Trade*

Use local organic milk — it's much better for both you and the planet, it will have traveled less distance than ordinary milk, and you'll be encouraging a more sustainable and healthy way of farming.

Mobile Phones

If your cell phone stops working, don't throw it away — get it repaired. There are many companies that will fix your cell at a very reasonable price; simply mail them your phone.

If it is beyond repair, recycle your cell phone. Raise money for your favorite charity and divert your piece of electronic waste away from the landfill.

In the United States, over 150 million mobile phones are purchased every year, and over 425,000 are thrown away every day.

Monitors – *see Computers*

Mouse Pads

Buy mouse pads made from recycled materials. They are fun, cool, and give you the opportunity to flaunt your "green" credentials.

New Construction – *see also Air Conditioning, Carpets, Curtains, Flooring, Furniture, Heating, Insulation, Lighting, Paints*

If you are lucky enough to be considering building a new office, now is your chance to have an energy-efficient office tailor-made.

With a new or refurbished building you have the opportunity to invest in renewable energy systems, superb insulation, well-designed windows that allow sufficient natural light in but don't overheat the office in the summer, energy-efficient heating, natural cooling and ventilation, and so on.

Your designated Environmental Taskforce can play a key part in collating suggestions and ideas from other members of staff and presenting them to senior management. Although the initial construction costs might be a little higher, these expenses will soon be recouped through much lower energy bills. This is also an ideal opportunity to benefit from some very positive PR.

Notepads

Make office notepads from paper already printed on one side. Cut the sheets down to size and hold together with a metal clip.

Office Equipment – *see also Binding Machines, Computers, Laminators, Laptops, Photocopiers, Printers, Scanners*

It is currently estimated that over 1.5 billion pounds of e-waste is discarded in the United States every year, and this figure is on the increase.

When purchasing electrical equipment, compare running costs and energy use while on standby. Check that it has standby or power-down modes and other energy-saving features.

If your equipment is not too old, it can probably be refurbished and reused. Check out the Internet for reuse and recycling centers near you.

TRAFFIC-LIGHT SYSTEM

This system works well for electrical office equipment. Simple colored stickers in a prominent position on all electrical machines show employees whether machines should be left on or turned off. Make people aware of the system by poster or e-mail.

GREEN — use for machines that can be switched off when not in use — rather than letting them go into standby mode. Most office computers will be green.

AMBER — use for machines that are best left switched on during the day, as they take a long time to warm up, but can be switched off at the end of the day. Photocopiers are a good example of equipment that will be marked amber.

RED — is for equipment that has to be kept turned on all the time. Office answering machines and wax printers are typical red-coded machines.

Order Confirmation

Use e-mail rather than paper where possible.

Order Forms – *see also Invoices, Statements*

Consider using electronic order forms instead of paper; you can create them as PDF documents and e-mail them to customers. You could also suggest to your customers that they use the same system.

Orders – *see Couriers, Deliveries, Order Forms*

Organic – *see also Coffee, Fair Trade, Kitchens, Tea*

Support organic farmers and encourage a more pleasant and healthy way of farming. Pesticides and fungicides sprayed onto produce are potentially harmful to the farmer, the planet, and you the consumer. Reduce your exposure to such chemicals by choosing to eat and drink organic produce. Organic tea, coffee, and milk are now readily available.

Packing Materials – *see also Paper*

- Organize your office with bins to collect all the packing materials you receive, so that you can reuse them. Collapse and flat-pack cardboard boxes until required for reuse

- If you receive more packing material than you can reuse, don't throw it away — donate your surplus to other local companies

- Use starch-based, biodegradable packing peanuts (white foamlike extrusions) for shipping. They dissolve in water, are nontoxic, and can be composted

- Avoid using expanded polystyrene and plastic wrapping — there is biodegradable cellulose available for shrink-wrapping if needed

- Reuse jiffy bags where possible, and if you purchase jiffy bags, choose ones that are lined with recycled paper rather than bubble wrap, as these can be recycled easily

Paints

Encourage the use of natural paints and wood finishes for your office. These are completely nontoxic, and contain no solvents or other poisonous by-products to pollute your office environment.

There is a vast array of environmentally friendly natural paints and associated products available to choose from.

Paper – *see also Forest Stewardship Council, Notepads, Packing Materials, Printing, Stationery*

Our consumption of paper in the United States continues to rise by about 20% every year.

Incredibly, and in spite of much publicity, we are still consuming ever-growing quantities of paper, so the paperless office has yet to become reality. Both the cutting down of trees for the production of virgin paper (which involves the use of a lot of energy and chemicals) and the disposal of paper waste, by either incineration or landfill, have high environmental costs.

The United States is one of the highest consumers of paper in the world, using more than 100 million tons of paper and cardboard every year, with this massive usage continuing to rise by about 20% annually. About half of all waste from an average office is paper. It is also a major cost, with many office workers using up to 100 sheets of paper daily. Reducing the paper consumption of your office will therefore have large environmental and financial benefits. It is also another "easy hit" target that, with an e-mail and poster campaign, can get most of the staff involved and motivated, and will produce quick, tangible results.

Reduce consumption

- Use e-mail, bulletin boards, LAN or intranet, rather than paper to communicate. Remind everybody not to print out e-mails unless absolutely necessary

- Encourage staff to use both sides of every sheet of paper. This should be possible for all printing and photocopying, with the exception of letters to clients

- Place posters or signs beside all printers and photocopiers reminding everybody to use both sides of the paper together with a "Do you really need to print this?" sign

- Put a recycling bin beside each machine to collect paper that can be used again; encourage this to be used in preference to virgin paper

- Edit standard letters to fit onto one page if possible

- Check out whether you could install a fax server. This would allow faxes to be sent directly from your PC, thereby avoiding the need to print out a copy. You can even set up your fax so that incoming faxes come into your PC digitally. You can then decide whether you need to print them out or simply forward the fax electronically to those concerned

- Make sure your fax is set up so that it does not produce unwanted report sheets

- Check out "Greenprint," a software program that analyzes what you intend printing, highlights and removes unwanted pages, and lets you decide what you really want to print. It also enables you to make PDFs at the click of a mouse thereby possibly removing the need to print **www.printgreener.com**

- Print your own letterheads and reduce the need to carry stock of letterhead paper. Company changes can be easily accommodated this way

- Use lighter-weight paper where possible — less energy and material are used in its manufacture

Recycle waste paper and reduce your disposal costs

- If you don't have your wastepaper collected for recycling, find out which companies collect paper for recycling near you. Costs and methods of collection vary, so clarify these before signing up

- Paper recycling bins need to be readily accessible to all staff. One beside every printer and photocopier is a good idea, and one additional bin for every six staff can be distributed around the offices

- As with all projects, its success depends upon ensuring that everyone is aware of what is happening and knows what to do. Posters beside the recycling bins providing explanations will help avoid problems

- Staff feedback is essential: use all means available to provide the opportunity for people to make suggestions and to report on progress and problems

- Ensure that all staff are kept informed of recycling progress; graphs and figures are a great way of saying "Look how well we're doing." For more suggestions, see page 6.

To make a ton of virgin paper you need as much electricity as an average household uses in a year.

Purchasing Paper

- Try to buy 100% recycled paper wherever possible, depending on your print requirements.

- If you need to reassure staff that recycled paper compares favorably with virgin paper, get some samples of different types of recycled paper and try them out before ordering

- Try to purchase recycled paper that has the highest "post-consumer waste" content. Terms you will come upon when ordering recycled paper include:

  - "Post-consumer waste" — wastepaper that has been collected from offices and homes to be recycled

- "Pre-consumer waste" — scrap paper created by paper mills and other paper-processing operations

- Try to use recycled paper that has been produced in an environmentally sensitive way. In particular, try to avoid the use of chlorine (used to bleach the pulp) as it is particularly damaging to the environment

- If you cannot get recycled paper to the specification you require, consider using FSC paper (see **Forest Stewardship Council** above)

The Paperless Office

You can reduce your paper use by:

- Using electronic methods for standard office procedures, e.g., invoices, statements, order forms — PDFs are generally used

- Filing documents electronically, backed up as necessary

- Encouraging others to reduce their paper use by putting a message at the end of your e-mails asking the recipient to avoid printing it if possible

- Using electronic planners and calendars

- Using your Web site to post documents for the general public and the media, e.g., reports, news

- Using a Local Area Network (LAN) to communicate with other staff members

- Sharing information securely over the Internet, for example using Googlemail documents and spreadsheets

Paper Towels – *see Kitchens, Restroooms*

Paperclips – *see Staples*

Pencils

There are pencils made from recycled materials, or get a pencil for life — i.e., one that has replaceable leads

Pens

Why not give a fountain pen a try? Those that don't use cartridges are the most eco-friendly, and can last for many years. However, for those who still prefer the instant, nonsmudge ballpoint pens, there are now huge ranges of pens and pencils, including marker pens, that are made from recycled materials and are biodegradable.

Ensure that the ink in the marker pens is nontoxic; it should be toluene-free and xylene-free. Check out refillable versions, and whether the supplier collects the "used and empty" pens for recycling.

Photocopiers – *see also Office Equipment, Printers, Traffic-Light System*

Most photocopiers can be included as part of the "amber" traffic-light-system group (see **Office Equipment**) as they are in frequent use and normally require a period to warm up. It's therefore generally best to leave them switched on during the day and switch them off before leaving for home. Photocopiers, like printers, are often used indiscriminately, and they waste paper. Put a bin for scrap — that is, paper that has been printed on both sides — and a box for paper that can be reused by the side of all photocopiers, and a couple of simple notices will help reduce paper use: "Do you really need a paper copy?" or "Use both sides of the paper if possible."

Planners – *see Calendars*

Plants – *see also Composting, Flowers, Gardens, Rain Barrels*

Use plants in your office to "green" your workplace. Plants have been found to be very effective at reducing air pollution in enclosed places (e.g., the spider plant, *Chlorophytum comosum*) they also act as excellent room dividers, as well as raising the

humidity of the air and deadening noise. Potted plants last longer than cut flowers; buy plants that have been grown locally rather than flown in from abroad. Plant air miles damage the environment, contributing to the carbon dioxide levels in our atmosphere and hence to climate change.

If you have some outdoor garden space, you can use this to grow your own office plants. Many benefit from a colder period outdoors prior to being brought inside, where they will flower, bringing color and "a breath of fresh air" to your office.

To avoid death by overwatering, make sure that one person is responsible for the care and maintenance of the office plants.

Plastic – see Celebrations, Christmas, Cups, Packing Materials, Pens

Waste plastic is a major problem for the environment, and much of it ends up in landfills. It is derived from oil, a nonrenewable resource. Offices traditionally use a lot of plastic product — for example, shrink-wrapping and polystyrene packing materials, both of which can easily be substituted with an environmentally friendly product. Where possible, use biodegradable products made from a renewable resource, or those that can be reused, rather than plastic.

Postage Meters – see also Stamps

There are now alternatives to postage meters: you can print your own stamps from the Web, which means one less machine running in your office, and which saves energy and money.

Posters – see also Environmental Taskforce

Judiciously placed posters around the office are an excellent means of informing staff about environmental projects, including successes, stories, media coverage, future events, and the like. If used in tandem with e-mail circulars, your Local Area Network (LAN) or the intranet, they provide frequent reminders and "keep people on board." However, ensure that the environmental-taskforce member responsible for posters keeps them alive and current. Tired, "dog-eared" posters can easily give the wrong message out to the staff. Fresh, lively posters with personal stories that seek to change habits by using a carrot rather than a stick are preferable. But beware of their overuse — this could be counterproductive, as the posters themselves require paper and printing.

Printers – *see also Binding Machines, Computers, Ink Cartridges, Laminators, Office Equipment, Paper, Photocopiers, Scanners*

Most printers can be included as part of the "amber" traffic-light-system group (see **Office Equipment**) as they are in frequent use and normally require a period to warm up. It's therefore generally best to leave them switched on during the day and switch them off before leaving for home. However, some wax printers are "red"-coded machines and need to be kept switched on all the time, so check this out before placing the appropriate "traffic-light symbol" onto the printer.

Encourage staff to utilize the "economy" or "speed" facility available when instructing the printer to operate from PCs (generally found under "print quality"). These modes use considerably less ink and are much quicker. Save "best" print quality for external communications.

See **Paper** for more information on how to reduce paper usage when printing.

Purchasing

When upgrading your printer, check to see that standby or power-down modes and other energy-saving features are included. Compare running and standby energy use before purchasing. Also check out the purchase price of the ink cartridges; see if they can be refilled or if remanufactured replacements are available.

Reuse and Recycle

Check out the Internet for reuse and recycling organizations near you. If your printer is not too old, it can probably be refurbished and reused elsewhere.

Promotional Literature – see also Training Manuals

Where possible use e-mail and the Web to promote your business to save paper.

Public Transportation – see Cars

Purchase Orders – see Order Forms

Rain Barrels

Water down the drain is wasted; if your office has a garden or outside space, collect free water from the roof by installing a rain barrel, and use this water for your plants inside and outside rather than using treated drinking water.

Recycling – see individual subjects

Recycling Bins – see also Cups, Envelopes, Kitchens, Packing Materials, Paper, Rubbish

Recycling is easy, but also needs to be made easy: place bins, clearly labeled, where they are needed and easily seen. For example:

- The kitchen and dining areas: check with your local officials or recycling collection company to see what they collect and how they would like it separated. A bin for metal cans, with another to collect certain types of plastics, would be great here

- Entrance lobby: the same types of bins as in the kitchen area can be placed here ready for staff coming back from lunch
- Next to printers and photocopiers: wastepaper bins, again clearly marked as such but with reminder signs such as "Have you used both sides?" placed on the bin. (See **Paper** above for further information)
- In shared office space: one wastepaper bin for about every six staff, again with similar reminders as above

Renewable Energy – *see also New Construction*

Renewable energy is energy produced by a source that continually renews itself; main sources are the sun, moving water, wind, and plant materials. This energy can be used for space heating and hot water, and to produce electricity for your office. By using renewable energy instead of conventional energy sources you will reduce your carbon footprint and thereby lessen the impact of climate change.

Solar power

Energy from the sun can be used both to provide domestic hot water and to produce electricity for your office. Different technologies are used for each.

Wind turbines

Wind turbines convert moving wind into electricity. It may be possible to install a new kind of microturbine that attaches to your office building's chimney or roof.

Biomass (biofuels)

Biomass or biofuels are materials such as wood or straw that grow quickly and can be burnt to release heat for space heating and domestic hot water. Biomass is different from all other renewable energy sources because the fuel generally has to be purchased.

Biomass is a renewable energy source because the materials are quick to grow, absorbing CO_2 in the process; and the CO_2 released when it is burnt balances that which was absorbed during the growth of the material, effectively making the process carbon-neutral.

Ground-source heat pumps

Heat pumps take heat from under the ground (which remains at about 54°F all year round) and use it to heat your office — just like a refrigerator in reverse. You will need sufficient space outside to dig either a trench or a borehole if you want to install a ground-source heat pump.

Small-scale hydropower

If you are fortunate enough to have a fast-moving stream or river running near your office, it may be possible to generate electricity from the moving water. Such hydro plants have the capacity to generate substantial amounts of electricity, which in some places can then be sold back to your electricity company.

Reports

Send reports by e-mail and/or put them on your Web site and invite people to download them.

Restrooms – see also Air Fresheners, Cleaning, Water

Toilets and sinks consume the majority of the water used in an office, and your office water bill will be a major expenditure. Simple water-efficiency measures allied with effective communications can reduce the water bill of your company by 50%.

• Install waterless urinals

- Install dual-flush toilets. The short flush will be used most of the time. If dual-flush toilets are not available, at least install low flow (1.6 gallons per flush)
- You can reduce the amount of water that your existing toilets use by fitting water-saving devices in the tanks
- Install push-button faucets on the sinks. These will cut your water usage by over 50%
- If your office has urinals that are not waterless, reduce your water consumption by fitting automatic flush controllers. The tanks will then only flush during office hours or after use
- If you use paper towels, buy recycled
- If you use electric hand dryers, position them so that they are not turned on by passing people
- Avoid air fresheners; use natural ventilation instead

Discuss with the company that cleans your office the use of environmentally friendly cleaning products for both your bathroom areas and the remainder of the office. Make sure that water coloring/foaming agents are not placed in the toilets — they are totally unnecessary and require additional treatment at the sewage treatment plant.

Ride Sharing – *see also Cars, Car Pools*

Can you travel with someone else, share costs, and save a trip?

Rubbish – *see also Recycling Bins*

An environmentally friendly office will have minimum waste to dispose of in landfills. Much can be recycled or reused (see the individual subject). Sensible purchasing will dramatically reduce waste and therefore disposal costs.

- If possible, ensure that the volume and/or weight of waste for disposal is noted and communicated to staff. Although

there are some waste products such as sanitary waste that will not diminish, it should be possible to dramatically reduce all other products requiring disposal

- Keep staff on board by informing them of goals attained, future targets, and possible prizes for high achievers
- Although it may seem slightly Orwellian, occasional bin checks when the office is empty will inform the Environmental Taskforce of weaknesses in the system

Scanners – *see also Office Equipment*

Most scanners are only used infrequently and therefore should be switched off when not in use, and should have a "green" sticker on them if you adopt the traffic-light system (*see* **Office Equipment** *above*).

However, if your office uses the scanner frequently and it takes a while to warm up, then it might warrant an "amber" traffic-light symbol.

Shredders

Ideally, use a manual shredder; you can use the shredded material that is not confidential as packing material.

Soap – *see Cleaning*

Solar Energy – *see Renewable Energy*

Solvents – *see also Cleaning, Furniture, Glues, Pens*

Toxic solvents that evaporate into the air are present in a surprising number of office products, and can damage your health. There are now environmentally friendly alternatives available — see individual topics for further information.

Stamps

Consider buying your postage online instead of using "stick on" stamps. **www.usps.com**

Staples

Staples are such small pieces of steel that they are easily ignored. Have a look at staple-less paper joiners, or use reusable paper clips instead.

Statements

Consider using electronic statements instead of paper; you can create your statements as PDF documents and e-mail them to customers.

Sticky Notes

Use electronic versions, recycled paper notepads, or buy recycled.

String

Use biodegradable (e.g., cotton, sisal, or jute) rather than plastic where possible.

Switch Off – *see also Lighting, Office Equipment*

This is the mantra of energy saving: switch off lights, heating, air conditioning, and other electrical devices when they are not in use. See the individual topics listed for further information, and check out the "traffic-light system" — see **Office Equipment**.

Tax Returns

Do them online, saving paper and money.

Taxis

Like all other cars, taxis emit CO_2 – can you use public transportation instead?

Tea – *see also Coffee, Composting, Kitchens, Milk, Organic*

Less carbon dioxide is emitted in organic farming — buy organic tea and use organic milk, ideally from a local source.

If a number of you make tea at the same time, how about using a teapot and using loose tea rather than tea bags? This way you will avoid the additional packaging required for tea bags and possible effects on your health from the bleaching agents used by some manufacturers to whiten the bags. If you still need to buy tea bags, then purchase the nonbleached variety.

Don't forget: when you've finished your tea you can compost the used tea leaves and tea bags. See **Composting** above for further information.

Telephone Directories – *see also Yellow Pages*

Use the Web to find telephone numbers. Be sure to recycle your old directories. Opt out of having telephone directories delivered by calling your local phone company.

Telephones

Try to avoid base stations, which have to be charged. There is currently a debate about the health issues surrounding cordless phones.

Tissues

Bring back the handkerchief!

Toner Cartridges – *see Ink Cartridges*

Traffic-Light System – *see Office Equipment*

A system that can be used for all electrical office equipment:

> RED = must be left turned on
> AMBER = put on standby
> GREEN = switch off when not in use

Training Manuals

If your company uses training manuals, put them on the LAN or intranet as a download or make them available on a CD. Phase out the use of hard copies, as they consume large quantities of paper and are soon out of date and then need reprinting. If you have to print hard copies, try to get them printed on recycled paper using vegetable inks and avoid having plastic laminates on the covers.

Trains

Use them!

Transportation – *see Cars, Company Cars, Cycling, Flights, Trains*

Trash – *see Rubbish*

Vending Machines – *see also Cups, Water Coolers*

Vending machines are left on all the time, quietly using energy; food and drink in these machines is almost never from a local source and therefore involves many food miles. Look into alternative ways of providing food and drink for the office, such as a sandwich-delivery service or a kitchen area. If you do lease a water cooler, make sure people use their own cups or glasses rather than disposables.

Ventilation – *see Air Conditioning, Windows*

Waste – *see Rubbish*

Water – *see also Kitchens, Restrooms*

Water is a significant proportion of your office expenditure, so reduce your water use and save money. Treating and pumping water to your office also requires huge amounts of electricity, so you reduce emissions of greenhouse gases responsible for climate change by using less water.

The majority of water used is in bathrooms and sinks, as well as in your office kitchen. See **Restrooms** and **Kitchens** above for detailed information on how to reduce water consumption in these areas.

A few simple water efficiency measures and effective communications can cut your water bill by 50%.

Water Coolers

These are similar in design to fridges and use considerable amounts of electricity, as they are never turned off. There are two types — those that use delivered bottles of water and those that are connected to the local water supply; avoid the additional CO_2 emissions associated with water miles and use the local variety. When renewing or starting a lease for a new water cooler, check out the electricity consumption of the various models and choose accordingly.

Wi-Fi

Although wireless networks are growing in popularity because of the lack of the need for wiring and ease of movement of equipment, there are concerns about long-term health implications of exposure to low-level electromagnetic radiation from wireless networks. Consider using conventional wiring for your office networks.

Wind Turbines – *see Renewable Energy*

Windows – *see Air Conditioning, Heating, Ventilation*

Yellow Pages – *see also Telephone Directories*

Use the Web to find telephone numbers. Be sure to recycle your old directories. Opt out of having new directories delivered to the office.

Resources

Canada Green Building Council accelerates the design and construction of green buildings in Canada. The Council is a broad-based inclusive coalition of representatives from different segments of the design and building industry. **www.cagbc.org**

Energy Star is a rating system that ranks office products that meet or exceed energy-efficient guidelines. **www.energystar.gov**

The Environmentally Responsible Green Office at a Glance is a booklet produced by Public Works and Government Services Canada for use by Canadian government offices, but with checklists adaptable to others. **www.pwgsc.gc.ca/realproperty/ text/pubs_ercr_guidebook/toc-e.html**

The Forest Stewardship Council (FSC) promotes responsible management of the world's forests. It certifies products manufactured from virgin materials sourced from well-managed forests. **www.fscus.org**

www.greenbiz.com An online resource that covers all aspects of going green in the office, sponsored by Greener World Media. For specifics and a checklist go here: **www.greenbiz.com/ toolbox/essentials_third.cfm?LinkAdvID=15205**

Greenprint is free software that can help you save paper and toner. **www.printgreener.com/**

www.grinningplanet.com A Web site with jokes, cartoons, and useful articles about health, energy, and the environment. **www.grinningplanet.com/index.htm**

www.treehugger.com/ A resource for going green in all aspects of life, from health and home to office and transportation and beyond. **www.treehugger.com/**

The Mailing Preference Registry helps individuals and organizations to reduce junk mail. **www.directmail.com/ directory/mailpreference**